German – Russian

Favorite Recipes

Volume 2

Reuben A. Bauer
Author

Copyright Page

Heritage Books Canada
ISBN: 978-1-990265-01-3   Printed in Canada
Copyright © 2021 by Reuben A. Bauer
Author/ Editor: Bauer, Reuben A.
"Old Favorites of the German-Russian Recipes" Volume 2

Summary: This volume, like all the other volumes in this series of Volume 1 to 8, and future ones, are the compilation of good food recipes collected from mothers, grandmothers, and daughters over the centuries past who lived both in the Volga Region of Russia and then migrated to other parts of the world, namely Canada and the United States. Of these fore bearers, the descendants are the fortunate ones to inherit a legacy of richness in tasty foods, culture, and history. These recipes are a "must have" to complete the traditions of the past.

First edition: June 2009
Second edition: November 2009
Third edition: November 2010
Fourth edition: June 2011
Fifth edition: March 2021
Edmonton, Alberta, Canada

Heritage Books Canada
#374, 9768-170 St.
Edmonton, Alberta, Canada, T5T 5L4

ALL RIGHTS RESERVED: No part of this publication or any publication in this series may be reproduced in any language, stored in any retrieval system or transmitted, in any form or by any means, electronic, mechanical, photocopying, recording, or otherwise, without the written prior permission of the author and copyright holder.

Foreword

In this volume, like all the other seven volumes of the German-Russian Recipes, we see a refreshing selection of old favorite foods that have graced the dinner tables of German-Russian families for decades. Among these collections of "good eating" foods are the recipes that are authentic German dishes. Herein you will also find a sprinkling of other selected and well-used recipes that favored the German-Russian families.

All these recipes are the original or derivatives of German-Russian foods. In some cases, modifications have been made from the original recipes due in part to either to suit the taste and/or availability of ingredients of the German-Russian housewives, mothers, and grandmothers during the last 250 years, plus. In their migration from Germany, these people brought with them as much as they could to settle in their new home along Russia's Volga River region.

We are proud to offer up these authentic and tasty foods in these people's spirit and culture. Many of these were staple dishes chosen for the week-day eating and the Sunday best by the grandmothers, daughters, and granddaughters in every household. The Volga German-Russian colonists made their home along the Steppes of the Volga River region, often referred to as the "bread-basket" of Mother

Russia. The settlement took root as early as 1763 and consisted of 103 colonies.

Join us as we give thanks to God for their lives and examples they were to the millions of their descendants worldwide, even to this day. Join us also in one of the many prayers of "blessing" that were spoken at the tables before they broke bread and participated in, as well as the prayers of "thanksgiving" offered after eating their delicious and hearty foods.

Throughout this book and all the other eight volumes are the many prayers used in these families' homes in the original German language and translated into English where possible. Accompanying the prayers are some especially fitting proverbs.

Contents

Copyright Page 2
Foreword 4
Soup 10
    DEUTSCHE HOCHZEIT SUPPEE 10
    DRIED FRUIT SOUP 12
    CZAR'S EGG DROP SOUP 13
    KARTOFFEL SUPPEE 14
    BORSCHT SUPPEE 15
    CHEESY CHEDDAR CHOWDER 16
    HUMBURGER GERMŰSEE SUPPEE 17
Salads 18
    KRAUT SALATE 18
    LEMON AND ORANGE SALAD 19
    SINFUL SALAD 20
    HEAVENLY SALAD 21
    3-WEEK COLE SLAW 22
    CAULIFLOWER SALAD 23
    TACO SALAD 24
    FROZEN FRUIT SALAD 25
Main Dishes Und Casseroles 26
    RINDERROULADEN 26
    CHEESY BROCCOLI BAKE 27
    QUICK CHILI 28
    HAMBURGER-ONION PIE 29
    CHICKEN–RICE STIR-FRY 30

 GERMAN ROAST 31
 CHICKEN AND VEGETABLE BAKE 32
 FAULE PEROHAY 33
 LAYERED CHICKEN HOTDISH 34
 HONEY GARLIC CHICKEN WINGS........................35
 HONEY GARLIC SAUCE 35
 BEROK OR KRAUT KUCHEN..................................36
 DOUGH 37
 KÄSEE STRUDEL 38
 GERMAN SMOTHERED CHICKEN........................39
 SPANISH RICE 40

Breads 41
 FAVORITE DATE AND NUT BREAD 41
 POTATO BUNS 42
 ZUCCHINI LOAF 43
 RIVVELL KUCHEN..44
 WHOLE WHEAT BREAD 45
 KARTOFFEL BROT 46

Muffins 47
 BLUEBERRY MUFFINS 47
 CREAM MUFFINS..48
 PLAIN OLD MUFFINS 49

Rolls 50
 OBERDORF COFFEE CAKE 50
 BUTTER ROLLS 51
 QUICK PECAN ROLLS..52
 PEPPER SPICE ROLLS..53

DEENA KUCHEN MIT RIEBBLE 54
Bleena 55
   BLINNA 55
Pancakes 56
   CORNMEAL PANCAKES 56
   TANTA WEITZEL'S PANNEKUCHEN 58
   FRUIT SYRUP FOR WAFFLES AND PANCAKES
   59
Cakes 60
   GRAHAM TORTE 60
   GERMAN CHOCOLATE CAKE 61
   COCONUT PECAN FROSTING 62
   CHOCOLATE NUT ZUCCHINI CAKE 63
   ENGEL KUCHEN 64
Cookies 65
   FAT MAN'S COOKIES 65
   SAUCE PAN CHEWS 66
   PUMPKIN COOKIES 67
   RUM MAKRONENSPEISE 68
Desserts 70
   LEMON PUDDING 70
   RICE PUDDING 70
   CORN CHEESE PUDDING 72
   GLORIFIED RICE DESSERT 73
   SQUAMISH BARS 74
Pies 75
   RHUBARB PIE 75

CHEESE PIE 76
CHOCOLATE RUM PIE 77
GERMAN COCONUT CREAM PIE 78
Grebbles 79
ZUGGER GREBBEL 79
BUTTERMILK GREBBLES 80
VESSY NATALA GREBBLES 81
GREBBLES MIT SŰSSE MILCH 82
DOUGHNUTS RAISED 83
Glössé 84
HAM AND POTATO DUMPLINGS 84
POTATO NOODLES DUMPLINGS 85
SCHLAG GLŐSSÉ 86
PFLAMEN GLASSÉ 87
THIS AND THAT'S 88
HOMEMADE VANILLA 88
FRUIT SYRUP for WAFFLES AND PANCAKES ... 89
TOPPING WITH MERINQUE 89
MAKING "RIEVAL" TOPPINGS FOR COFFEE CAKES 90
HOW TO MAKE CHOCOLATE CANDY 91
CANDIED WALNUTS 92
PASCKA (Russian) 93
PASKA (German) 94
MAKING HOMEMADE NOODLES FROM SCRATCH 95
BENEFITS OF HONEY AND CINNAMON 97

Soup

DEUTSCHE HOCHZEIT SUPPEE
(German Wedding Soup)

6 chicken breasts
6 c. water
3 chicken bouillon cubes
1½ lbs. ground beef
3 Tbsp. bread crumbs
1 Tbsp. parsley
2 Tbsp. Parmesan cheese
¼ tsp. Pepper
1½ tsp. Salt
2-10 oz. Pkg. frozen chopped spinach

Method:
Place chicken breast in water and cook covered for about 30 min., or until tender. Remove chicken from the soup pot and shred. Return to the soup pot and add the chicken bouillon cubes. Bring to a boil. In the meantime, combine beef, crumbs, parsley, cheese, salt, and pepper. Mix well. Shape into marble or grape size balls. Drop these dumplings

into boiling broth. Cook for 30 minutes. Add spinach. Cook for 10 min. longer. (Serves 12) (Double the ingredients for a larger feast.) (NOTE: Brown meatballs in the oven slightly before adding to soup (about 10 min. at 375 *F.) You can also add a small type of pasta to thicken the soup.

[This soup was the traditional soup used for most all German-Russian weddings in most colonies of Russia.]

DRIED FRUIT SOUP

(*This soup is usually eaten on Good Friday and Easter, as it contains no meats.*)

1 lb. mixed dried fruits
1 cup raisins
3 qt. cold water
1 pt. sweet or sour cream
¼ c. sugar (or to taste)
2 Tbsp. Flour
½ tsp. Baking soda
½ c. cold water
3 Tbsp. butter

Method:

Wash dried fruits and raisins thoroughly. Add cold water and boil for 1 hour. Make a paste of flour, soda, and ½ cup cold water. Remove sour from heat and add paste slowly, stirring. Add a small amount of soup mixture to the cream, stirring constantly. Add the rest of the cream to the soup and heat through. Do not boil. Add butter and sugar.

CZAR'S EGG DROP SOUP

4 c. chicken broth or stock
¼ c. green onions, finely sliced
1 Tbsp. gingerroot, minced
½ c. cooked chicken, finely chopped
½ c. frozen peas, thawed
2 Tbsp. soy sauce
1 egg

Method:

Using a medium saucepan, combine chicken broth, green onion, gingerroot, chicken, peas and soy sauce. Bring to a boil, then reduce heat to low. In a 1 cup, beat egg thoroughly with a fork or whisk. Slowly pour egg into HOT soup in a steady stream, using a circular motion. Egg cooks right away. Serve immediately to the Czar in your household.

KARTOFFEL SUPPEE
(Potato Soup)

3 to 4 medium potatoes, diced
Water, enough to cover potatoes
1 tsp. minced onion
½ bay leaf
1 egg, slightly beaten
¼ c. half and half
Salt and pepper to taste

Method:
Boil potatoes, onion and seasonings in water till tender, add slightly beaten egg slowly to soup mixture. Cool another minute or two and add half and half (or thin cream). Ready to serve.

BORSCHT SUPPEE
(Beet Soup)

2 lbs. beef chuck
1 qt. beets, cut into julienne strips
1 small onion, chopped
1 bay leaf
5 whole allspice
salt to taste

Method:
Put all ingredients, except beets in a large pot. Cover with water. Simmer slowly for an hour. Then add beets and cook until beets are tender. Just before serving stir in ½ cup sour cream. Remove from heat. Serves 4.

Salads

KRAUT SALATE
(Cabbage Salad)

Slice cabbage thinly (as for a slaw)
½ stick of butter, heated in skillet
Add sliced onion and simmer on low heat until just tender
Add 1/3 c. vinegar
¼ c. water,
1 Tbsp. sugar
Add salt and pepper to taste.

Method:
Just before serving add ½ pint light cream

LEMON AND ORANGE SALAD

1 large pkg. lemon or orange Jello
1 c. hot water
1 small Can frozen juice (orange)
½ c. cold water

Method:
Place in the refrigerator until firm. Beat 1 kg. Dream whip and add to it when nearly set. You may add chopped fruit, nuts, or marshmallows.

SINFUL SALAD

1 lg. strawberry Jello
1 c. boiling water
3 medium mashed bananas (1 cup)
1 c. chopped pecans
1 c. (20 oz. can) pineapple, drained
1 medium container sour cream
2 (10 oz.) can strawberries, thawed and drained

Method:

Combine gelatine and boiling water. Stir with rubber spatula. Cool. Add bananas, pecans, strawberries, and pineapple to gelatine and stir to combine. Divide in half. Pour ½ in a 12x8 inch pan. Refrigerate until set. Spread sour cream over and cover with remaining ½ gelatine mixture. Cover and set at least 1½ hours.

HEAVENLY SALAD

1 pkg. lime Jello
¼ c. sugar
¾ c. hot water
1 sm. Pkg. curd cottage cheese (11 oz.)
1 c. whipping cream
¼ c. maraschino cherries, cut up (red and green)
½ c. nuts (optional)

Method:

Dissolve Jello in hot water, cool and add sugar. When congealed, fold in cottage cheese, whipped cream, cherries and nuts. Pour into mold and chill till firm.

3-WEEK COLE SLAW

3 lbs. grated white cabbage
1 green pepper, chopped
2 c. sugar

Combine and mix well.

Bring the following to hard boil:
1 c. oil
1 c. vinegar
2 Tbsp. celery seeds
1 Tbsp. salt

Method:
Pour over cabbage mixture; stir well. Store in refrigerator in sealed container for 3 days. Will keep for a month, refrigerated.

CAULIFLOWER SALAD

1 head lettuce
1 head cauliflower
1 lb. bacon
2 c. mayonnaise
¼ c. sugar
½ c. Parmesan cheese

Method:
Break into pieces the lettuce, cauliflower and bacon. Combine the mayonnaise, sugar and Parmesan cheese and toss all together.

TACO SALAD

1 lb. ground beef
1 packet taco seasoning
½ c. water
1 head of lettuce, chopped
1 can kidney beans, drained
1 tomato, chopped
2 c. cheddar cheese
Onions (optional)
1 large bag of Doritos, crushed
1 bottle dressing (your choice)

Method:

Brown ground beef; drain. Add taco seasoning and water; simmer. In large bowl combine all ingredients, including ground beef mixture. Serve.

FROZEN FRUIT SALAD

- 5 oranges
- 5 bananas
- 1 small can pineapple
- 1 c. whipped cream
- 1 small bottle maraschino cherries
- 1 c. cooked salad dressing

Method:
Blend all ingredients, turn into mold and chill several hours. Serve on crisp lettuce with little salad dressing.

Main Dishes Und Casseroles

RINDERROULADEN
(German Round Steak Roast)

4 oz. bacon, diced
4 oz. onion, diced
1 round steak, 1/8" thick, cut into 4 pieces (or 4 thin slices sirloin steak)
mustard
salt and pepper
3 oz. fat
1-2 tsp. flour

Method:

Cook bacon slightly, set aside. Cook onion until barely translucent, set aside. Spread steak with mustard, salt and pepper. Add bacon and onion. Roll like jelly roll. Secure with skewers and / or string. Brown well on all sides in heated fat. Add 1 cup water. Cover and cook slowly 2-2½ hours on top of stove or in 325*F. oven, turning often, adding water if necessary. Remove from pan, place on serving platter and keep warm. Stir flour and water into meat juices and make gravy. Season to taste. Pour over rouladen and serve hot. Yield is 4 servings. (Suggestion: Paprika, lemon, tomato paste or heavy cream may be added to gravy.)

CHEESY BROCCOLI BAKE

1 (10-oz.) pkg. frozen broccoli
1 (10¾ oz.) can creamy chicken soup
1 c. chicken or turkey, cooked and cubed
1 c. cooked rice
1 c. grated American cheese
½ c. sour cream
½ c. buttered crumbs, or crumbled potato chips

Method:

Preheat oven to 350*F. Cook broccoli until tender, drain well. Stir together soup, sour cream. Add remaining ingredients to soup, sour cream mixture. Spoon in 1½ - quart casserole. Sprinkle with crumbs. Bake 30-35 minutes. Serves 4-6.

QUICK CHILI

2 cans (14 oz.) stewed tomatoes, Mexican style
1 can (14 oz.) tomato sauce
2 cans red kidney beans
1 lb. ground beef, browned & seasoned to taste

Method:
Mix in cooking pot and simmer 30 minutes. Then serve.

HAMBURGER-ONION PIE

Mix 1 cup Bisquick (biscuit mix) and ¼ to 1/3 cup milk. Knead 10 times on board lightly dusted with Bisquick. Roll and place in 9-inch pan.

Sauté:
1 lb. ground beef
2 medium onions (sliced)

Add:
1 tsp. salt
½ tsp. flavor extender
¼ tsp. pepper
2 Tbsp. Bisquick

Method:
Spread in pan. Beat 2 eggs. Mix with 1 cup cottage cheese. Pour over meat. Sprinkle with paprika. Bake at 375*F for 30 minutes.

CHICKEN–RICE STIR-FRY

1 clove garlic (minced)
2 Tbsp. oil
1½ c. cooked chicken, ham pork or beef, cut up
1 (20-oz.) pkg. frozen oriental vegetables (thawed)
2 c. fresh mushrooms
½ red or green pepper (optional)
2 c. water
1½ c. Minute Rice
Soy sauce to taste

Method:
Sauté garlic in oil in electric frying pan or wok until browned. Add meat, raw pepper, vegetables, mushrooms and water, and bring to a boil over high heat. Sir in rice, cover, turn off heat and let stand 5 minutes; add soy sauce before serving. Serves 6.

GERMAN ROAST

- 2 lbs. beef
- 2 qt. Water
- 1 Tbsp. salt
- 3 bay leaves
- ½ tsp. mixed spices
- 2 large onions

Method:

Combine all ingredients in a large kettle and cook until well done. Remove meat from kettle and place in roaster with potatoes and carrots around it. Pour broth over all and reserve some for basting. Roast in oven set 375*F. for 2 hours.

CHICKEN AND VEGETABLE BAKE

6 skinless, boneless chicken breast pieces
3 potatoes, chopped (leave skins on)
2-3 carrots, chopped
1 medium onion, chopped
¾ c. Zesty Italian dressing
Parmesan cheese

Method:
Place chicken and vegetables in large baking dish. Drizzle with dressing. Cover with foil. Bake at 400*F. for 1½ hours. During last 10 minutes of baking, remove foil.

FAULE PEROHAY
(Lazy Perogy Casserole)

15 lasagna noodles
2 c. cottage cheese
1 egg
¼ tsp. onion salt
1 c. margarine
2 c. mashed potatoes
1/8 tsp. pepper
1 c. onion, chopped
1 c. Cheddar cheese, grated
¼ lb. bacon, cooked and diced

Method:

Cook noodles as directed on pkg. Drain. Line bottom of a 9 x13 inch pan with first layer of noodles. In a bowl mix cottage cheese, egg, and onion, salt and spread over first noodle layer. Cover with second noodle layer. In a bowl, mix cheddar cheese, potatoes, onion salt, and pepper. Spread mixture over noodles. Cover with third layer of noodles. Sauté onion in frying pan with margarine until onions are clear and soft. Add bacon pieces and pour over noodles. Bake covered for 30 minutes at 350*F. Let sit 10 minutes before serving.

LAYERED CHICKEN HOTDISH

3 c. cooked chicken (or turkey)
1 medium bag frozen broccoli (cool & drain)
Velvetta cheese slices
2 cans cream of celery soup
2 small pkg. stove top stuffing, prepare according to directions

Method:

In a 9 x 13 pan layer chicken, drained broccoli, cheese slices; then spread soup carefully over slices. Top with prepared stove top stuffing. Bake at 350*F. for 35 – 45 minutes. Do not cover.

HONEY GARLIC CHICKEN WINGS

2 lbs. chicken wings – tips discarded, (separate into drummies and wingettes)
½ c. liquid honey
1/3 c. soya sauce
5 cloves garlic, sliced

Method:

Preheat oven to 325*F. Place wings in covered roasting pan and cook 30 minutes. Drain fat, toss with sauce mixture and cook uncovered for about 1¼ hours, turning wings every 20 minutes. Wings are done when they are richly glazed and honey is no longer liquid. For more intense garlic flavor, add garlic in last half hour of cooking.

HONEY GARLIC SAUCE

½ c. honey
1 c. ketchup
¼ c. soya sauce
4 cloves garlic, crushed

Method:

Heat until smooth and everything is mixed together. Great over chicken or meatballs.

BEROK OR KRAUT KUCHEN
(Meat and Cabbage Bread)
A Full Meal in itself

3 or 4 lbs. beef shank
3 onions, diced
1 c. cooking oil
1 or 2 heads of cabbage, shredded

Method:

Boil beef, season to taste with onion, bay leaf, salt and pepper and make soup with it. When tender, cool and grind meat in coarse grinder (cooked pork or chicken may be added, if desired). Fry onions and cabbage until tender, stirring all the while, not to brown. Cool and mix with meat. Season to taste about 2/3 cabbage to 1/3 meat.

(Continued on the next page)

DOUGH

1 c. half and half, scalded, cooled
1/3 c. thick sour cream
1 c. potato water cooled
4 eggs, beaten lightly
7 to 7½ c. flour
½ c. sugar
1 Tbsp. salt
1 pkg. dry yeast in
1/3 c. warm water
1/3 c. butter

Method:

Mix in order given and medium dough. Pour butter around edge of dough and let rise until double twice. Knead down lightly each time. When it has risen the third time, take out one-third dough on floured board and roll out about ¼ inch thick. Cut in 4 – inch squares; put apart a little, fill each square with one heaping tablespoon of meat filling and fold pastry over, pressing edge tightly. Turn the pressed side to the bottom and shape into oblong squares. Put on greased cookie sheet 2 inches apart and brush with butter or cream. Let rise about 25 minutes. Bake at 350*F for 25 minutes or until golden brown. Remove from pan and place on cooling racks. Brush with cream. A full meal in itself when served with soup, tea or coffee.

KÄSEE STRUDEL
(Cheese Strudel)

3½ c. flour
1 tsp. salt
1½ lbs. dry cottage cheese
5 eggs
¾ c. water
1½ Tbsp. sugar
1 small onion
5 Tbsp. hot bacon grease

Method:

Combine flour, salt, 2 eggs, ¾ c. water. Knead well and place dish upside down over the dough for 1½ hours. Roll out on board about 1/5 of the dough at a time. Roll out and place 1 tablespoon of hot bacon grease on it. Pull and stretch out dough as thin as possible without tearing it. The secret is to get it paper thin and almost transparent. Mix cottage cheese with 3 eggs, salt, pepper to taste. Add sugar. Mix and spread a portion on the thin dough sparingly, rolling up as a jelly roll. In a frying pan have 3 tablespoons of lard or bacon drippings, onion, ¾ cup water. Place roll into this and cover with tight lid. Don not lift lid for 25 minutes. Cook on medium hear till all water has evaporated and you can hear it frying crisply. Remove and cut in pieces to serve.

GERMAN SMOTHERED CHICKEN

1 chicken
1 pkg. dried chicken noodle soup
1 can milk
1 medium onion, sliced

Method:
Brown chicken. Spoon off drippings, then sprinkle on dried soup. Mix around chicken pieces. Add ½ cup of water (or more) and the onion. Cover and cook over low heat for 30- 35 minutes until tender. Place chicken in a deep serving dish. Stir in can of milk into liquid left in skillet. Cook and stir until steaming hot but do not boil. Pour sauce around chicken in serving dish.

SPANISH RICE

1 c. uncooked rice
4 Tbsp. oil
1 onion, sliced
1 green pepper
1/8 tsp marjoram
1 slice garlic
4 c. canned tomatoes
2 tsp. salt
1 tsp. chili powder

Method:
Wash, drain and dry rise thoroughly. Heat oil in heavy frying pan and cook rice, stirring constantly, until light brown. Add sliced onion, pepper and garlic, and continue cooking about 5 minutes. Transfer to casserole. Heat tomatoes with seasonings and pour over rice, mixing well. Cover and bake in 350*F oven for about 45 minutes, until rice is tender and liquid gone. Do not stir while cooking. Serve with vegetables like peas, carrots and perhaps corn if desired.

Breads

FAVORITE DATE AND NUT BREAD

1 c. chopped dates
1 tsp. soda
¾ c. boiling water
1 egg
¾ c. brown sugar
¼ c. melted shortening
1 tsp. vanilla
1½ c. flour
1 tsp. baking powder
1 tsp. salt
2/3 c. chopped walnuts

Method:

Stone and cut dates. Place in bowl and add soda. Pour over boiling water. Mix well. Let stand until cool. Beat egg until light. Add sugar gradually, beating between additions. Add salt and vanilla. Combine with date mixture. Add sifted dry ingredients and floured nuts. Add melted, but not hot, shortening. Mix well. Bake in well greased bread pan in 300 to 325*F oven.

POTATO BUNS
(Gramma Honstein Kartofel Brotchen)

1 c. mashed potatoes
4 c. flour
1 c. sugar
1 qt. warm milk
1 c. shortening
1 cake yeast soaked in
¼ cup warm water

Method:
Mix mashed potatoes and sugar; stir in milk and yeast. Add flour and mix well. Add melted shortening and mix well. Let stand 1 hour. Add 2 teaspoons baking powder, 1 tablespoon salt and another sifter of flour to the mixture and mix well. Let rise till bowl is full. Roll out half of dough on floured board, ½ inch thick. Cut with bun cutter and place on greased baking sheet 2 inches apart. Let raise 2 hours. Bake sheet 2 inches apart. Let rise for 2 hours. Bake in 375*F oven 15 to 20 minutes until light brown.

ZUCCHINI LOAF

- 2 c. flour
- 2 tsp. baking soda
- 1 tsp. cinnamon
- 1 c. oil
- 2 c. raw zucchini, grated
- 2 c. sugar
- 1 tsp. baking powder
- 3 eggs
- 2 tsp. vanilla

Method:
Blend sugar, oil, eggs and vanilla. Add dry ingredients. Then add zucchini.

Add:
- 1 c. raisins
- 1 c. walnuts, chopped

Place in greased loaf pans. Bake at 350*F. for 1 hour or 45 minutes in a 9 x 13 pan.

RIVVELL KUCHEN
(Coffee Cake with Crumbles)

Method:
To make the dough for the coffee cake here are the ingredients:

Dissolve 1 tablespoon yeast, 1 teaspoon sugar in ¼ cup warm water. Heat 1 cup buttermilk until lukewarm, add ¼ teaspoon soda to the milk and stir. Beat 1 egg, ¼ cup oil, ¼ cup sugar, 1 teaspoon salt and yeast. Add 2 cups flour and beat until batter is smooth. Add about 2 more cups of flour and knead until smooth. Set in warm place to rise until double in bulk. Roll out to fit into your pans. This makes two 10 x 14 kuchens. Let rise until double in bulk, top with your favorite topping. (See below how to make Rivvells for topping). A fruit topping takes about 35 minutes to make.

Rivvell Topping:
- 1 egg beaten
- 2 Tbsp. sugar
- 2 Tbsp. cream
- 1 Tbsp. flour

Method:
Beat ingredients together, moisten your hands, and crumble the mixture until you have fine crumbly consistency. Spread over dough made and in pans.

WHOLE WHEAT BREAD

1½ c. lukewarm water
1½ c. milk, scald and cool
3 Tbsp. butter, melted
3 Tbsp. brown sugar
1½ tsp. salt
1 cake yeast
2½ c. coarse whole wheat flour, sifted
2½ c. medium whole wheat flour, sifted
2½ c. fine whole wheat flour

Method:

Dissolve yeast, sugar in lukewarm water. Add butter, scalded milk, salt. Add coarse flour, mix well, add rest of lour, keep dough soft. Place in well-greased bowl in warm place, let rise double its bulk. Form in 2 loaves, place in well-greased pans, set to rise 1 hour. Bake 1 hour in slower oven than white bread, at 350*F in greased loaf pan.

KARTOFFEL BROT
(Potato Bread)

4-5 lbs. old potatoes
pinch of salt
3-4 c. flour

Method:
Boil potatoes with salt, then mash while warm. To make the dough, add flour and work with hands, adding enough flour to make soft dough. Form into 4 balls. Roll on flour board to 1/8 inch thickness and cut in 8 triangles. Cook in warm-to-hot frying pan until browned on both sides.

To serve: Usually as a breakfast dish.... Fry in oil or bacon fat a few minutes and serve with bacon and eggs.

Muffins

BLUEBERRY MUFFINS

2 c. flour
1 tsp. salt
1 c. milk
¼ c. shortening, melted
¼ c. sugar
1 egg
1 c. blueberries
3 tsp. baking powder

Method:

Sift dry ingredients. Beat egg and add milk, shortening, and blueberries. Stir into flour mixture; mixing only until flour is moistened. Fill greased muffin tins 2/3 full. Sprinkle sugar on top. Bake 425* F, for 15-20 minutes.

CREAM MUFFINS

1 egg
1¼ c. cream
2 c. flour, sifted
¼ tsp. salt
3 tsp. baking powder
2 Tbsp. sugar

Method:
Sift together the dry ingredients. Beat egg well, stir in the cream, then add the flour mixture. Fill buttered muffin tins two thirds full and bake about 20 to 25 minutes in a hot oven 425*F. This will make approximately 1 dozen.

PLAIN OLD MUFFINS

2 eggs
1 c. milk
4 Tbsp butter (or ¼ c. butter)
2 c. flour, sifted
3 tsp. baking powder
½ tsp. salt
2 Tbsp. sugar

Method:

Sift together the dry ingredients. Add the lightly beaten eggs and blend quickly to a smooth mixture. Pour into well-greased muffin tins and bake 20 to 25 minutes in a 425*F oven. If you want to dress up this recipe, here is what you can add.

Raisin Muffins... may be made using above recipe and adding ¾ cup raisins rubbed with little of the flour.

Date Muffins .... Use ¾ cup cut dates blended with a little of the sifted flour.

Berry Muffins .... Use ¾ cup canned berries, drain off juice. Blend with flour.

Rolls

OBERDORF COFFEE CAKE
(Quick Recipe)

(Make a smooth dough as you would for any bread dough.) Also use the recipe for the making of baking powder biscuits as ingredients shown below. Mix well using as much flour as needed.

¼ c. sugar
1 egg yolk, beaten
milk
baking powder
flour

Topping:
3 Tbsp. butter
¼ c. sifted flour
¼ c. sugar
1 tsp. cinnamon
½ tsp. vanilla

Method:
Here is where you Rievals for the topping. First you make a smooth dough for the base. Spread ½ inch thickness in a greased 9 inch square pan. Blend topping and spread over dough. Bake in a 400*F oven about 30 minutes. Your coffee cake should be ready.

BUTTER ROLLS

1 c. milk
½ c. sugar
4½ c. flour
½ c. shortening
1 cake yeast
1 tsp. salt

Method:

If dry yeast is used, use ¾ cup milk and ¼ cup water. Scald milk, add shortening, sugar and salt. Cool to lukewarm. Add crumbled yeast and mix. Then add flour. Mix smooth soft dough. Knead down once and let rise again. Knead second time and let rise to double the bulk. Put into pans. Let rise to double in size. Now bake for 20 minutes, at 375*F. Ready to eat.

QUICK PECAN ROLLS

½ c. light brown sugar
7 Tbsp. butter
1¼ tsp. cinnamon
½ c. cut pecans
use recipe for "baking powder biscuit" dough

Method:

Prepare Baking Powder Biscuit dough as (seen in the chapter "This and That's" of this book). Turn the dough on a lightly floured board and roll to ¼ inch thickness. Spread the dough with soft butter. Sprinkle with ½ cup light brown sugar and cinnamon. Roll like jelly roll and cut in pieces ½ inch thick. In the boot of the baking pan, melt butter, add light brown sugar and cut pecans. Place the rolls cut side down and bake in a hot oven, 400*F 20 to 25 minutes.

PEPPER SPICE ROLLS
(German Pfefferneece)

5 to 6 c. flour
2 pkgs. yeast dissolved in about 1½ c. water (let rise)
Add 1 c. sugar
1 tsp. salt
1 c. sour cream
1 c. molasses
flour enough to make a soft dough
1 tsp. black pepper
1 c. nuts (or 3 Tbsp. shortening

Method:
Let rise once kneaded down. Let rise once more. Then make into rolls. Let rise until light. Bake 375*F. or 20-25 minutes.

DEENA KUCHEN MIT RIEBBLE
(Coffee Cake with Riebbles)

1 pkg. dry granular yeast
2 eggs, beaten
7 Tbsp. butter, melted
4 c. flour, sifted
½ c. sugar
1 c. scalded milk (or ½ c. evaporated milk)
½ c. warm water
½ c. sour cream
1 tsp. salt

Method:
Beat eggs and add sugar and lukewarm milk and butter. Stir in yeast; stir well; stir in flour and salt. Pour into 2 pans and let rise in warm place until double in bulk for 1 hour. Put on riebbles or any other topping. (See "This and That's section in back of this book to making riebbles). Bake at 350*F for about 30 minutes.

Bleena (Flapjacks, Crepes)

(There are spelling variations for Bleena, beleena, blinna, blintzee)

BLINNA

2 c. flour
1 tsp. salt
¾ pkg. dry yeast dissolved in ½ c. luke warm water
1 Tbsp. sugar, rounded

Method:

Sift flour, sugar and salt. Make sponge with water as much as needed. Add yeast. Let set over night. Scald ½ cup milk, add ½ teaspoon soda and add to sponge and mix. Beat 2 eggs and add to batter, add to sponge. Let set a few minutes. Heat skillet, brush lightly with Crisco shortening. Put about a dipper full batter (small) on one side of skillet and let batter flow around skillet. When Blinna is somewhat dry turn, and bake until golden brown. Put on warmed plate and brush with hot melted butter. Continue baking the Blinna, keep warm in oven. Always brush each Blinna with butter as you proceed baking. Batter can be made in morning for luncheon or supper dish.

Pancakes

CORNMEAL PANCAKES

1½ c. yellow cornmeal
1 tsp. soda
1 tsp. salt
2 Tbsp. oil
1 egg white, beaten till stiff
¼ c. flour
1 tsp. sugar

2 c. buttermilk
1 egg yolk, beaten

Method:

Stir together cornmeal, flour, soda, sugar, and salt. Add buttermilk, oil and yolk. Blend well. Fold in egg white. Let batter stand 10 minutes. Bake on hot griddle, turning once.

TANTA WEITZEL'S PANNEKUCHEN

(Aunty Weitzel's Pancakes)
(*The Weitzel family were residents of the Norka Village on the Volga*)

½ lb. lean bacon slices or ham strips, cut in halves
6 eggs
½ c. milk
½ tsp. salt
2 Tbsp. flour
2 Tbsp. chopped chives

Method:

In heavy skillet, cook bacon until crisp, drain on paper towel, keep warm in oven. Drain all but 2 tablespoons of bacon grease from pan. Beat eggs until fluffy, beat in milk and salt and sprinkle in flour. Reheat pan with reserved bacon grease, pour in all the batter to cover entire surface. Turn heat to low, cook until batter is firm about 15-20 minutes, like a custard, then sprinkle with chives and bacon slices. Cut in wedges and serve hot.

FRUIT SYRUP FOR WAFFLES AND PANCAKES

1 c. brown sugar
½ c. corn syrup
1 c. fruit juice

Method:
Boil 3 minutes. Add your favorite canned diced fruit. Serve hot.

Cakes (Kuchen)

GRAHAM TORTE

2 c. graham cracker crumbs
1 c. milk
1 c. ground walnuts
2 tsp. baking powder
3 eggs
½ c. butter
1 c. sugar
1 tsp. flour

Method:
Cream butter and sugar; add eggs, one at a time and cream thoroughly after each addition; add milk and crumbs, nuts and flour. Bake in two cake tins in moderate oven.

Filling:
½ c. sugar
1 tsp. flour
1 egg yolk
½ c. milk
1 tsp. vanilla

Method:
Mix all the ingredients and cook until thick. When cool, spread between cake layers. Serve with whipped topping or any cake frosting desired.

GERMAN CHOCOLATE CAKE

6-oz. pkg. sweet cooking chocolate (or ¾ c. semi-sweet bits)
½ c. boiling water
½ c. margarine (or butter)
2 c. sugar
4 egg yolks unbeaten
1 tsp. vanilla
2½ c. sifted cake flour
1 tsp. baking soda
¼ tsp. salt
1 c. buttermilk
4 egg whites, stiffly beaten

Method:

Melt chocolate in ¼ cup boiling water. Cool. Cream butter and sugar till light and fluffy. Add egg yolks, one at a time, beating after each. Add vanilla and choclate and mix well. Sift flour with soda and salt. Add sifted dry ingredients alternately with buttermilk, beating until batter is smooth. Fold in stiffly beaten egg whites. Pour batter into three, 8 or 9 inch layer pans, lines on bottom with paper. Bake at 350*F for 35 to 40 minutes. Cool. Frost with Coconut Pecan Frosting (see below)

COCONUT PECAN FROSTING

- 1 c. evaporated milk (or half and half)
- 1 c. sugar
- 3 egg yolks
- ½ c. butter
- 1 tsp. vanilla
- 1 can tender-thin flaked coconut
- 1 c. chopped pecans

Method:

Combine milk, sugar, egg yolks, butter or margarine, and vanilla in saucepan. Cook over medium heat 12 minutes, stirring constantly, until mixture thickens. Add coconut and pecans. Beat until cool and spreading consistency. Makes enough to cover tops of three 9 inch layers. Do not frost sides of cake.

CHOCOLATE NUT ZUCCHINI CAKE

- 4 squares unsweetened chocolate
- 3 c. all purpose flour
- 1½ tsp. baking powder
- 1 tsp. baking soda
- 1 tsp. salt
- 4 eggs
- 3 c. sugar
- 1½ c. salad oil
- 3 c. grated zucchini
- 1 c. finely chopped nuts (optional)

Method:

Melt chocolate over hot water in double boiler. Let cool. Heat oven to 350*F. Grease and flour a 10 inch tube or bundt pan. Beat eggs, oil sugar in large bowl. Sift flour, baking soda, baking powder and salt. Add melted chocolate to egg mixture along with the dry ingredients. Stir in grated zucchini and chopped nuts. Bake for 1 hour and 15 minutes. Cool in pan on wired rack for 15 minutes then removed from pan. This is like pound cake so it does not require an icing, however, a glaze is good on it. Slice thinly. Serve with ice cream or fruit. It freezes well, too.

ENGEL KUCHEN
(Angel Cake)

1 c. sifted cake flour
1 c. egg whites (8 to 10 eggs)
½ tsp. salt
¾ tsp. vanilla
¼ tsp. almond extract

Method:
Sift ¼ cup sugar and flour together 4 times. Beat egg whites, cream of tartar and salt to a still foam. Add remaining sugar, a little at a time, beating it in (preferably with a rotary beater). Add flavorings. Fold in flour, sifting a little at a time over egg white and sugar mixture. Pour into a large ungreased tube pan. Cut through batter with a spatula and remove large air bubbles. Bake in a slow oven, 275*F, 30 minutes. Raise heat to 300*F and bake 40-45 minutes longer. Remove from oven. Invert pan 1 hour.

Cookies (Gaschnickker)

Gaschnickker (German-Russian Volga term used in reference to Desserts, Sweets, Pies, Cookies, et…… the after glow to the main course)

FAT MAN'S COOKIES
(Fattigmann's Pletzchen)

3 egg yolks
¼ c. heavy cream
2 whole eggs
4 tsp. sugar
¼ tsp. ground cardamom
1 Tbsp. butter, melted
1 tsp. vanilla
1¼ c. flour

Method:

Beat eggs until lemon colored (up to 15 minutes). Combine sugar and cardamom, add gradually to eggs beating until light. Add butter, cream and vanilla. Gradually stir in flour until dough is just stiff enough to handle. Chill. Roll about 1/3 of dough at a time on a floured board until very thin. Cut in 2 inch long strips. Then cut crosswise at a slant to form a diamond shape. Slit dough at one point of diamond and bring opposite point through the slit. Fry in deep fat at 365* F. about one minute. Drain. May be dusted with icing sugar.

SAUCE PAN CHEWS

2 eggs
1 c. brown sugar
2½ c. Rice Krispies
1½ c. dates, chopped
Coconut
¼ tsp. salt
1/3 c. butter
1 c. walnuts, chopped
1 tsp. vanilla

Method:

Beat eggs and brown sugar together. Melt butter in skillet over low heat. Remove from heat. Stir in egg mixture and dates. Set back over low heat. Cook and stir 10 minutes. Remove from heat. Stir in vanilla and salt. Combine Rice Krispies and nuts in a bowl. Pour date mixture over. Blend well. Cool to lukewarm. Butter hands and shape into small balls and roll into coconut. Store in sealed containers.

PUMPKIN COOKIES

- 1 cup shortening
- 1 cup pumpkin
- 1 cup milk
- 2 whole eggs
- ½ tsp soda
- 2 tsp baking powder
- 1 tsp maple flavoring
- 1 cup brown sugar
- 3 cups flour

Method:
Mix all ingredients together with mixer. Bake at 400° for 10 minutes. Drop by tsp on sheet.

RUM MAKRONENSPEISE
(Rum Macaroon Cookies)

1 cup heavy cream
3 egg yolks
3 Tbsp sugar
1 Tbsp flour
¼ tsp salt
1 tsp vanilla extract
12 almond macaroons
¼ cup light rum flavoring
1 pt. fresh strawberries
2 egg whites
2 Tbsp sugar

Method:
Day before or early in day: Heat cream in double boiler until tiny bubbles appear around edge. In medium bowl beat yokes slightly; stir in 3 tbsp sugar, flour, salt. Slowly stir in cream. Return mixture to double boiler. Cook, stirring constantly, over hot, not boiling, water until thick enough to coat spoon. Pour in bowl at once and cool. Add vanilla. *Cover and refrigerate.*

At mealtime:
Crumble macaroons in bottom of 8 sherbet glasses. Pour 1½ teaspoons rum flavoring over each. Let stand few minutes; spoon berries on top. Beat egg whites frothy. Add 2 Tbsp sugar while beating still. Fold all but ½ cup whites into custard. Spoon ½ cup

custard over fruit in each glass; then top with reserved egg whites. Refrigerate until served. Makes 8 servings.

Desserts

LEMON PUDDING

3 eggs separated
1¼ cup sugar
½ cup flour
Juice & grated rind of 2 large lemons
1/4 tsp salt
2 cups milk
2 tbsp melted butter

Method:
Beat egg whites until still and add 1/4 cup sugar. Let set. Combine egg yolks, juice and grated rind. Add 3/4 cup sugar, flour and salt. Add milk and melted butter. Beat all together with egg beater. Add in egg whites. Stir until mixture is smooth. Grease casserole a little and pour pudding in. Set in a pan of hot water. Bake at 375°F for 30 to 40 minutes. Serve with whipped cream.

RICE PUDDING

2/3 c. water
pinch of salt (or 1/8 tsp.)
½ c. rice
4 c. milk
4 egg yolks, beaten

½ c. sugar
1 orange or lemon, grated peel of
1 tsp. vanilla
seedless grapes
cinnamon

Method:

Bring water to boil in covered pan. Add salt and rice, cover and cook 4 minutes on medium heat. Remove from heat; keep covered. Scald milk in large pot, then stir in cooked rice. Cook over low heat about 35 minutes, stirring occasionally. Remove from heat. Cream egg yolks with sugar; stir into rice. Stir in grated peel. Cook and stir constantly over low heat until thick and creamy. Remove from heat; stir in vanilla. In a large bowl or individual bowls, decorate with grapes, cut in half or whole, sprinkle with cinnamon and chill. Serves 6.

CORN CHEESE PUDDING

1 large or 2 small eggs
1/8 tsp. black pepper
1 Tbsp. cut parsley
¼ tsp. garlic salt
1 tsp. Worcestershire sauce
1 c. undiluted evaporated milk
1 pt. corn
1 tsp. salt
2 Tbsp. minced onion
1 Tbsp. finely chopped green pepper
dash of Tabasco sauce
1 c. cheddar cheese shredded

Method:

Whip eggs with fork, stir in seasonings and other ingredients. Turn into shallow baking dish. Top with thin slices of cheese. Bake at 325*F for about 40 minutes. Serves 6 people.

GLORIFIED RICE DESSERT

1 c. cold rice, cooked
1½ c. pineapple, crushed & drained
8 marsh mellows, cut up
½ c. sugar
1 c. whipping cream, whipped
1 small can mandarin oranges, drained

Method:
Mix all together and chill thoroughly. Please note, that a fruit cocktail can be used in place of or in addition to oranges.

SQUAMISH BARS

- ½ c. corn syrup
- ½ c. brown sugar
- 1 c. peanut butter
- 1 c. Rice Krispies
- 1 c. Corn Flakes
- ¼ c. butter
- 2 Tbsp. vanilla custard powder
- 3 Tbsp. milk
- 2 c. icing sugar
- 3 Tbsp. butter
- 3 squares semi-sweet chocolate

Method

Melt together corn syrup, brown sugar and peanut butter. Stir in cereals. Press into well-greased 9 x 9 inch pan. Refrigerate. Beat together the ¼ c. butter, custard powder and milk; blend in icing sugar. Spread over cooled base refrigerate. Melt butter and chocolate over low heat; spread evenly over filling. Keep refrigerated. Allow to stand at room temperature for 10 minutes before cutting. Cut with hot, wet knife to avoid chocolate cover from breaking up unevenly.

Pies

RHUBARB PIE

2 Tbsp. flour
1 c. sugar
½ tsp. salt
1 egg
2 c. rhubarb
1 Tbsp. butter

Method:

Beat egg. Add sugar, flour, salt and then add rhubarb. Mix. Place in unbaked pie shell. Bake at 450*F. for 10 minutes, decrease to 350*F. for 40 minutes.

CHEESE PIE

36 graham crackers, crushed fine
1 Tbsp powdered sugar
1 cube butter
1 can evaporated milk, chilled
1 large pkg. cream cheese
1 small pkg. cream cheese
1 c. sugar
1 Tbsp. vanilla
1 pkg. lemon Jello

Method:
Roll crackers fine (save some for topping); add sugar and melted butter and put in pie tine for crust. Mix Jello with ¾ cup boiling water; cool. Whip chilled milk; add cold Jello (not jelled) to it. Fold in whipped cream cheese, sugar and vanilla. Four mixture into 2 pie shells; sprinkle with reserved cracker crumbs.

CHOCOLATE RUM PIE

1 pkg. Nestle's chocolate
1 egg
2 eggs, separated
1 Tbsp. rum (or 1 tsp. vanilla)
1 c. whipping cream

Method:
Melt chocolate over hot water; remove from heat and add 1 who egg. Mix well. Add yolks one at a time, beating well after each addition. Add flavoring (rum or vanilla). Whip egg whites, also cream; fold the two together and add to chocolate, folding in gently. Four in baked pie shell and chill several hours. Serve with whipped cream and lots of it.

GERMAN COCONUT CREAM PIE

5 Tbsp. coconut dessert
5 Tbsp. sugar
1/8 tsp salt
½ c. cold water
1 baked pie shell
1½ c. scalded milk
3 egg yolks
1 c. shredded coconut
2 tsp. vanilla

Method:

Blend coconut dessert with the cold water, then slowly add ½ cup of the hot milk and mix well. Add sugar and beaten egg yolks blended together. Cook in double boiler until thick. Add shredded coconut and cook 3 minutes. Cool and add vanilla. Pour into baked pie shell and cover with meringue made of stilly beaten whites of 2 eggs and 3 tablespoons granulated sugar, ¼ teaspoon vanilla. Sprinkle top with ½ cup shredded coconut. Return pie to oven to lightly brown.

Grebbles (German Doughnuts)

(Grebles, grebbel, grebbles, krepple were a type of German-Russian doughnut. Each family and village had their own special kind of Grebble and ingredients to match. The spelling of the word differed from village to village.)

ZUGGER GREBBEL
(Sugar Doughnuts)

oil for deep frying (as much as needed)
- ¼ c. sugar
- 2 Tbsp. butter
- 2 eggs, beaten
- 2/3 c. milk
- 1 tsp. vanilla
- 2 c. flour
- 2 tsp. baking powder
- ½ tsp. salt
- ½ tsp. nutmeg

Coating:
- ½ c. sugar
- ½ tsp. cinnamon

Method:

Heat oil to 375*F. Beat sugar and butter into beaten eggs. Add milk and vanilla. Sift dry ingredients and blend well with butter mixture. Use a teaspoon to drop dough into hot oil Fry until dark or golden brown. Drain and let cool. Combine sugar and cinnamon. Roll well-drained doughnut ball into sugar mixture. Serve warm or cooled.

BUTTERMILK GREBBLES

3 eggs, lightly beaten
½ cube butter (or margarine melted)
1 c. buttermilk
3 c. unsifted flour
½ tsp. Baking powder
½ tsp. baking soda
1 tsp. salt
1 tsp. sugar

Method:

Beat eggs lightly, add margarine (or butter) and buttermilk. Put flour right on top of liquid. Add other dry ingredients on top of flour. Mix with a fork and then with your hands. Let set a few hours at room temperature. Roll out on floured board to about ¼ inch thick. Cut into rectangular shape. Make a slit in the center. Twist one end through the slit, then fry in very hot oil (deep). They will brown quickly. Turn them over once and when they are light brown on either side remove from oil. Take note that they should not burn too dark. Place on tray lined with paper towel. Sprinkle with sugar.

VESSY NATALA GREBBLES
(Little Aunty Natalie's Doughnuts)

1 pt. sour cream
½ c. buttermilk
4 eggs beaten
½ c. sugar
1 level Tbsp. salt
1 tsp. baking powder
½ tsp. baking soda
5 c. flour

Method:
Sift flour once before measuring. Sift twice together with salt, baking powder and baking soda. Add sugar to dry ingredients. Combine beaten eggs, buttermilk and sour cream and add to flour. Roll out on floured board to approximately ¼ inches thickness. Cut in strip 2 inches x 5 inches or any size desired. Cut a slit in center of each strip and bring to ends together. Any shape may be used. You may wish to twist them if you like. Fry in deep fat. Dough can be stored overnight in refrigerator if necessary.

GREBBLES MIT SŰSSE MILCH
(Doughnuts with Sweet Milk)

3 eggs, beat well
1 c. sugar
3 Tbsp. butter, melted
1 tsp. salt
1 c. milk
3½ c. sifted flour
4 tsp. baking powder, well rounded
1 tsp. vanilla
½ tsp. nutmeg

Method:

Beat eggs using rotary whisk. Beat in sugar. Stir in milk. Add sifted dry ingredients, melted butter. (This dough is soft, but the doughnuts are light.) With knife toss one third of dough on floured board, knead lightly. Roll to ¼ inch thickness. Use floured knife to prevent sticking. Use flour cutter. Fry in deep hot fat for 2 to 3 minutes then turn often, cool 4 to 5 doughnuts, at a time. Drain on brown paper after removing from fryer. While fried doughnuts are still warm dip them in granulated sugar and garnish with multi-color sprinkles.

DOUGHNUTS RAISED

2 c. sweet milk
1 c. mashed potatoes
1 c. sugar
1 c. warm water
1 tsp. salt
4 Tbsp. lard
4 eggs
1 cake yeast

Method:

Put yeast in water for ½ hour before using. Add enough flour to make a soft dough. Heat milk add lard, massed potatoes, sugar and salt. Cool. Add yeast that was put into water. Add enough flour to make soft dough. Punch dough 2 times, then roll out, cut and let raise. Fry in hot oil until browned on both sides. Remove and dip melt chocolate or icing sugar as a garnish.

Glössé (Dumplings)

(Glössé, glace, gleese, kleasel, glöessé, klössé were the different spellings for this word. Each family and village had their own special kind of Dumplings and ingredients to match. The spelling of the word differed from village to village.)

HAM AND POTATO DUMPLINGS

6 medium potatoes
1 c. diced ham or bacon
1 medium sized onion
3 c. flour
2 eggs

Method:

Boil potatoes. Dice ham and onion and fry golden brown. Mash potatoes; add 2 teaspoons salt and pepper. This is the filling. Mix 3 cups flour, 2 eggs, 3 tablespoons water. Knead on flour board. Roll out 1/8 inch thick; cut in 4 inch squares. Put 2 large tablespoons filling on each square. Pinch all four corners together tightly. Put the dumplings in 2 quarts boiling water, salted, and boil 5 minutes. Remove from water. Place in bowl and pour ½ cup cream and 1 cup boiling water which dumplings were boiled in, and pour over. Melt 2 tablespoons butter; add cracker or bread crumbs and let brown. Pour over dumplings. Can fry in deep fat. Serves 4

POTATO NOODLES DUMPLINGS

2 large potatoes, cooked and mashed
1 medium sized onion, sliced

Method:
Melt 2 tablespoons shortening, add sliced onion and brown. Add potatoes, Season.

Dough:
2 eggs,
2 Tbsp. water
1 tsp. salt.

Method
Add enough flour to make stiff dough. Roll thin and cut in squares 3 x 3½ inches. Place 1 tablespoon potato mixture on each square. Pinch dough tight around filling. Drop in deep kettle of boiling water, salted. Boil 10 minutes or until they float. Remove and place in deep serving bowl. Top with 2 tablespoons melted butter and browned bread crumbs. Pour ½ pint cream (heated) over noodles and serve.

SCHLAG GLŐSSÉ

½ cube butter
2 eggs
pinch of salt
pinch of nutmeg
enough flour

Method:

Melt ½ cube of butter; beat in 2 eggs. Add a pinch of salt, pinch of nutmeg; mix well. Now add enough flour for making a soft dumpling dough. Rub this mixture in your bare hands until it is Rivvelly. Put ½ teaspoon of Rivvells into soup broth, one at a time. Do not stir broth. Boil broth for 8 to 10 minutes. Then serve. (See back section of this book on making Rivvells under "This and That's".

PFLAMEN GLASSÉ
(Plum Dumplings)

4 baking potatoes
2 egg yolks
1 tsp. salt
1 Tbsp. butter
2 c. flour (approximately)
2 lbs. plums (or apricots)
1 sugar cube
¼ tsp. cinnamon
buttered bread crumbs
½ tsp. sugar

Method

Boil potatoes in skins. Peel, mash and chill. Mix in egg yolks, salt and butter. Add half of flour and knead, adding more flour as needed until dough is smooth and resilient. Roll into long sausage-like rolls, about 1 inch diameter. Slice into 1½ inch pieces. Cut fruit just enough to remove pits, replace pit with sugar cube and press together. Wrap dough around fruit and press edges to seal. Cook in rapidly boiling water 15 minutes, or until dumplings rise to the surface. Reduce heat and simmer 10 minutes longer. Remove with slotted spoon; drain. Roll in bread crumbs browned in butter. Sprinkle with sugar and cinnamon, if desired. Serves 6.

THIS AND THAT'S

German-Russian ladies in the homemade kitchens did not have store-bought vanilla. There were no corner grocery stores, like we have today, to which they could go and buy this ingredient for baking. They had to make their own brand of vanilla. Here is how to make your own vanilla.

HOMEMADE VANILLA

1 vanilla bean, chopped
½ tsp. sugar
3 oz. vodka

Method:

Put in a jar, cover tightly, shake well every day for a month. It is then ready to use.

FRUIT SYRUP for WAFFLES AND PANCAKES

1 c. brown sugar
½ c. corn syrup
1 c. fruit juice

Method:
Boil 3 minutes. Add your favorite canned fruit diced. Serve hot.

TOPPING WITH MERINQUE

¼ tsp. Cream of tartar
4 Tbsp. Sugar
2 egg whites
½ tsp. Vanilla

Method:
Now be prepared to whip first of all the 3 ingredients until soft peaks form Gradually add sugar until all is dissolved and meringue is glossy. Bake at 350*F. for 12 – 15 minutes. (For a larger amount of meringue, use 3 egg whites and 6 Tbsp. of sugar.

MAKING "RIEVAL" TOPPINGS FOR COFFEE CAKES

1 c. flour
1 cube butter, melted in saucepan
½ c. sugar

Method:
Add flour and sugar to butter with hand or spoon. Mix until coarse, crumbly mixture develops. This becomes the topping used on most all German Coffee Cakes.

HOW TO MAKE CHOCOLATE CANDY

1 lb. milk chocolate
1 c. broken walnut pieces
½ lb. fresh marshmallows

Method:

Melt chocolate in double boiler over warm water. (Water should be no hotter than is comfortable to the hand) Stir occasionally. Into a 8 inch greased pan, cut marshmallows. Sprinkle nuts over marshmallows and mix thoroughly. When chocolate is melted (about 45 minutes later) pour over other mixture. Allow to stand 6 to 8 hours. Yields about 1 ¾ pounds of candy.

CANDIED WALNUTS

1½ c. sugar
½ c. water
¼ c. honey
½ tsp. Vanilla

Method:
Stir and boil to 245*F on candy thermometer or soft ball stage. Remove from heat; add ½ teaspoon vanilla and 3 cups crisp walnut halves, (or cashews, peanuts, almonds, etc.). Stir until thick and creamy, pour into greased pan. Separate with 2 forks.
Makes 1½ pounds. (Cinnamon or grated orange rind may be added.)

PASCKA (Russian)
(Specially for Easter)

4 large pkgs. Philadelphia cream cheese
¼ c. butter (1 cube), melted
½ c. sour cream
1 c. candied fruit, chopped fine
4 Tbsp. sugar
1 pkg. chopped almonds
½ c. raisins

Method:
Mix above ingredients well, adding one at a time. Shape mixture into a pyramid like mold to become firm. To keep moist and from drying out, place a wet cheese cloth into the mold before putting in the mixture. As this pyramid like box is upside down like a **V** shape, the mixture is poured in from the wide end. Place in a refrigerator to keep cool. Place some heavy weights on the pascka in frame so it will set well. Before you remove the frame, place it on your favorite big plate, remove wooden mold or frame, then remove cheese cloth. Some families, would decorate the pascka with tiny pieces of colorful Easter candy eggs or chocolate chips. Then serve.
(*This mold was usually handmade with ¼" plywood or boards with a symbol carved on each inside frame:* **cross**, **ladder**, **egg** *and* **tree**. *Usually this pascka was prepared a day or two a head of Good Friday, so it was ready to eat on Good Friday and throughout the Easter weekend including Easter Sunday.*) These symbols had special meaning for the church family. The cross signified the death of Christ, the ladder signified the Ressurection of Christ, the egg signified the new life and rebirth in Christ and the tree was the "tree of life" which God gave mankind in which to grow and be fruitful and multiply.

PASKA (German)
(Specially for Easter Celebration)

3 lbs. dry cottage cheese
½ lb. butter
1 ¼ c. sugar
1 c. whipping cream, (thick farm cream)
3 egg yolks
½ tsp. salt
1 tsp. vanilla (or rum flavoring)
1 c. white raisins (or dark raisins)
¾ c. mixed candied fruit (optional)

Method:
Put cottage cheese through ricer. Have butter at room temperature. Beat cream with fork until frothy. Thoroughly mix cottage cheese, butter, eggs, cream, sugar, salt and flavoring. Add raisins and fruit. Put into wooden form.(See description above.) If form is not available, punch hole in bottom and side a 2 pound coffee can. Line the container with cheese cloth and fill to top. Put small plate on top so it will fit inside can. Weigh down with heavy bottle, medium sized rock, or jar filled with water. Set into refrigerator for 24 hours. Unmold and serve.

Das Blut' Jesus Christus
Macht uns rein
Von allen Sünden. Amen.

The blood of Jesus Christ
Will purify us
From all our sins. Amen

MAKING HOMEMADE NOODLES FROM SCRATCH

(This recipe for making home made egg noodles was done in the villages of Norka and Odessa from which were sent to us by descendants of those communities.)

3 eggs, beaten
2 Tbsp. milk
2 c. white flour
1 tsp. salt

Method:

Combine all ingredients and mix well. (May require more milk than this.), to make a stiff dough. Roll very thinly. Roll up the dough, like you would for a jelly-roll and then cut noodles from the roll, with a sharp knife. Before cutting the roll of dough, let stand in a covered bowl with a tea towel for an hour. Then roll. Cutting each roll very thinly at an angle, pressing with one hand on the roll to keep it firm, until all is cut. To help dry the noodles, toss them up and fluff to let them air out. When sufficiently dry place them in a plastic bag and put in refrigerator for an hour or longer for use in soups or casseroles. Be prepared to put them into a chicken broth ready for the soup.

HOW TO MAKE "BAKING POWDER BISCUITS"

2 c. flour, sifted
4 tsp. baking powder
½ tsp. salt
4 Tbsp. butter (or other shortening)
2 c. flour, sifted
4 tsp. baking powder
½ tsp. salt
4 Tbsp. butter (or other shortening)
¾ c. milk

Method:

Sift flour, measure, add salt, baking powder, and sift again. Cut in shortening (butter), gradually add milk and make into a soft dough. Roll one half inch thickness with little flour on board, cut with floured biscuit cutter and bake in hot oven about 15 minutes at 450*F.

BENEFITS OF HONEY AND CINNAMON

As we know that honey, (in its natural form) is a food source that does not spoil. The German-Russians used honey and cinnamon, nutmeg, paprika and cayenne pepper with great frequency in their cooking and normal medicines. As the grandmothers did most of the cooking and baking, and the daughters and daughters-in-law were busy raising and nurturing their children, the grandmothers knew all these old recipes and remedies for health and survival.

As you will see in many of the German-Russian recipes, honey is used as a substitute for sugar as a sweetening agent. Besides, cinnamon was used so frequently in cooking and baking as a natural seasoning and for the health benefits that these ingredients had was truly marvelous.

In the latter years, we have taken this for granted and largely ignored these remedies, as old fashioned and "old wives tales". I have taken the liberty to give you the age-old remedies used by the grandmothers down through the ages with great success. Many current studies now reveal that these old recipes and remedies to be more valuable, practical and beneficial for health and survival than previously thought to be so. As modern-day medicines were unknown and unavailable to many of these German-Russian people.

It is found that a mixture of Honey and Cinnamon cures most of the diseases. Honey is produced in most of the countries of the world. German-Russians, as a cultural group, have been using these mixtures of honey and other seasonings as a vital medicine for centuries. Scientists of today also accept honey as a very effective medicine for all kinds of diseases. Honey can be used without any side effects for any kind of diseases. Today's science says that even though honey is sweet, if taken in the right dosage as a medicine, it does not harm even the diabetic patients.

HEART DISEASES: Make a paste of honey and cinnamon powder, apply on bread, toast or other breads, instead of jelly and jam and eat it regularly for breakfast. It reduces the cholesterol in the arteries and saves the patient from heart attack. Also those who already had an attack, if they do this process daily, they are kept miles away from the next attack.

Regular use of the above process relieves loss of breath and strengthens the heartbeat. In the United States and Canada, various nursing homes have treated patients successfully and have found that as age the arteries and veins lose their flexibility and get clogged; honey and cinnamon revitalizes the arteries and veins.

INSECT BITES: Take one part honey to two parts of lukewarm water and add a small teaspoon of cinnamon powder, make a paste and massage it on the itching part of the body slowly. It is noticed that the pain recedes within a minute or two.

ARTHRITIS: Arthritis patients may take daily, morning and night, one cup of hot water with two spoons of honey and one small teaspoon of cinnamon powder. If taken regularly even chronic arthritis can be cured.

In a recent research conducted at the Copenhagen University, it was found that when the doctors treated their patients with a mixture of one tablespoon Honey and half teaspoon Cinnamon powder before breakfast, they found that within a week out of the 200 people so treated practically 73 patients were totally relieved of pain and within a month, mostly all the patients who could not walk or move around because of arthritis started walking without pain.

HAIR LOSS: Those suffering from hair loss or baldness, may apply a paste of hot olive oil, one tablespoon of honey, one teaspoon of cinnamon powder before bath and keep it for approx. 15 min. and then wash the hair. It was found to be effective even if kept on for 5 minutes.

BLADDER INFECTIONS: Take two tablespoons of cinnamon powder and one teaspoon of honey in a glass of lukewarm water and drink it. It destroys the germs in the bladder.

TOOTHACHE: Make a paste of one teaspoon of cinnamon powder and five teaspoons of honey and apply on the aching tooth. This may be applied 3 times a day till the tooth stops aching.

CHOLESTEROL: Two tablespoons of honey and three teaspoons of Cinnamon Powder mixed in 16 ounces of tea water, given to a cholesterol patient, was found to reduce the level of cholesterol in the blood by 10% within 2 hours. As mentioned for arthritic patients, if taken 3 times a day, any Chronic cholesterol is cured.

As per information received in the said journal, pure honey taken with food daily relieves complaints of cholesterol.

COLDS: Those suffering from common or severe colds should take one tablespoon lukewarm honey with 1/4 spoon cinnamon powder daily for 3 days. This process will cure most chronic cough, cold and clear the sinuses.

INFERTILITY: German-Russian grandmothers often used this honey mixture to strengthen the semen of men. If impotent men regularly take two tablespoon of honey before going to sleep, their problem will be solved.

Today in China, Japan and Far-East countries, women, who do not conceive and need to strengthen the uterus, have been taking cinnamon powder for centuries. Women who cannot conceive may take a pinch of cinnamon powder in half teaspoon of honey and apply it on the gums frequently throughout the day, so that it slowly mixes with the saliva and enters the body.

UPSET STOMACH: Honey taken with cinnamon powder cures stomachache and also clears stomach ulcers from the root.

GAS: According to the studies done in India & Japan, it is revealed that if honey is taken with cinnamon powder the stomach is relieved of gas.

IMMUNE SYSTEM: Daily use of honey and cinnamon powder strengthens the immune system and protects the body from bacteria and viral attacks. Scientists have found that honey has various vitamins and iron in large amounts. Constant use of honey strengthens the white blood corpuscles to fight bacteria and viral diseases.

INDIGESTION: Cinnamon powder sprinkled on two tablespoons of honey taken before food, relieves acidity and digests the heaviest of meals.

INFLUENZA: A scientist in Spain has proved that honey contains a natural ingredient, which kills the influenza germs and saves the patient from flu.

LONGEVITY: Tea made with honey and cinnamon powder, when taken regularly arrests the ravages of old age. Take 4 spoons of honey, 1 spoon of cinnamon powder and 3 cups of water and boil to make like tea. Drink 1/4 cup, 3 to 4 times a day. It keeps the skin fresh and soft and arrests old age.

Life spans also increases and even a 100 year old, starts performing the chores of a 20-year-old.

PIMPLES: Three tablespoons of Honey and one teaspoon of cinnamon powder paste. Apply this paste on the pimples before sleeping and wash it next morning with warm water. If done daily for two weeks, it removes pimples from the root.

SKIN INFECTIONS: Applying honey and cinnamon powder in equal parts on the affected parts cures eczema, ringworm and all types of skin infections.

CANCER: Recent research in Japan and Australia has revealed that advanced cancer of the stomach and bones have been cured successfully. Patients suffering from these kinds of cancer should daily take one tablespoon of honey with one teaspoon of cinnamon powder for one month 3 times a day.

FATIGUE: Recent studies have shown that the sugar content of honey is more helpful rather than being detrimental to the strength of the body. Senior citizens, who take honey and cinnamon power in equal parts, are more alert and flexible.

Dr. Milton who has done research says that a half tablespoon honey taken in a glass of water and sprinkled with cinnamon powder, taken daily after brushing and in the afternoon at about 3.00 p.m. when the vitality of the body starts to decrease, increases the vitality of the body within a week.

BAD BREATH: People of South America, first thing in the morning gargle with one teaspoon of honey and cinnamon powder mixed in hot water. So their breath stays fresh throughout the day.

HEARING LOSS: Daily morning and night honey and cinnamon powder taken in equal parts restore hearing.

*NOTE: The honey used needs to be **REAL RAW UNPASTEURIZED HONEY**. If it says PURE honey it is most likely pasteurized. It is best to only **buy honey that says RAW or UNPASTEURIZED** on the label. The difference is that the enzymes are all heated out of the pasteurized honey.

Cinnamon and Honey Formula for Weight Loss:

This should be prepared at night before going to bed.

1. Use 1 part cinnamon to 2 parts raw honey. 1/2 tsp cinnamon to 1 tsp honey is recommended but can use more or less as long as in the ratio of 1 to 2.... so 1 tsp. cinnamon to 2 tsp. raw honey is ok too, as an example.

2. Boil 1 cup...that is 8 oz of water.

3. Pour water over cinnamon and cover and let it steep for 1/2 hour. (30 minutes)

4. Add honey now that it has cooled. Never add honey when it is hot as the heat will destroy the enzymes and other nutrients in the raw honey.

5. Drink 1/2 of this directly before going to bed. The other 1/2 should be covered and refrigerated.

6. In the morning drink the other half that you refrigerated...but do not re-heat it...drink it cold or at room temp only.

Do not add anything else to this recipe. No lemon, no lime, no vinegar. It is not necessary to drink it more time in a day...it is only effective on an empty stomach and primarily at night.

This works for most people. Inches are lost before any measurement on the scales. This program will cause significant inches lost...but you will reach a plateau and may not lose anymore. This is because the cinnamon and honey cause a cleansing effect in the digestive tract and cleans out parasites and other fungus and bacteria that slow down the digestion...causing a toxic build up. (Lowers pH) Once this is all cleaned out then you will most likely have the weight loss slow down.

Other side effects from a cleansing can occur because of toxins being released...if this occurs, cut back on how much you use or take a break.

Additionally people report increased energy, more sex drive, and feeling happier/mood enhancer.

www.ingramcontent.com/pod-product-compliance
Lightning Source LLC
Chambersburg PA
CBHW071741090426
42738CB00011B/2533